PRAISE FOR *KEEP MOVING*

"*Keep Moving* offers a bouquet of generosities in one hand, and a bouquet of soft but firm honesty in the other . . . A promise that what doesn't get better sometimes gets easier. And that, too, is worthy of celebration."

—Hanif Abdurraqib, author of *Go Ahead in the Rain: Notes to a Tribe Called Quest*

"I read this book in one sitting during one of the most difficult weeks of my life . . . This isn't lofty self-help stuff; she doesn't speak from above. Instead, she speaks next to you, whispering right in your ear that we are all in the trenches together. Every single page of this book made me breathe a little deeper and feel a little less alone."

—Amanda Palmer, singer, songwriter, musician, author of *The Art of Asking*

"Candid, lyrical, and full of empathy, this is a book that feels vital and welcome in these times . . . A stunning and wise piece of work."

—Sinéad Gleeson, author of *Constellations*

"Maggie Smith's mantras are a faithful and forgiving companion, coaxing us through the darkness and toward our own resilience."

—Rebecca Soffer, coauthor of *Modern Loss*

"I wish I'd had a copy of *Keep Moving* when my first marriage ended. It would have consoled my fears about being alone. Maggie Smith writes so honestly without being brutal, and she shows readers hope while avoiding the saccharine. To experience relief from a book is a rare and wonderful thing. *Keep Moving* gave me that relief."

—Bella Mackie, author of *Jog On*

"Maggie Smith's voice is the one I hear in my head, the one that keeps me going when I don't feel I can. And now, with this book, she has gifted the entire world with that particular brand of magic."

—Jennifer Pastiloff, author of *On Being Human*

"I lived this book in real time. I was going through something hard and heartbreaking . . . and every day I'd log on to social media . . . [to] read what you now hold in your hands: truth and pain and empathy and the wisdom that comes with living. We keep moving. I kept moving. So can you. I will carry copies of this beautiful gift of a book in my pockets and give them to everyone I know."

—Megan Stielstra, author of *The Wrong Way to Save Your Life*

Good Bones
The Well Speaks of Its Own Poison
Lamp of the Body

KEEP MOVING

———

*Notes on Loss, Creativity,
and Change*

———

MAGGIE SMITH

ONE SIGNAL
PUBLISHERS

———

ATRIA

NEW YORK   LONDON   TORONTO   SYDNEY   NEW DELHI

ONE SIGNAL
PUBLISHERS

ATRIA

An Imprint of Simon & Schuster, Inc.
1230 Avenue of the Americas
New York, NY 10020

First One Signal Publishers/Atria Books hardcover edition May 2020

ONE SIGNAL PUBLISHERS / ATRIA BOOKS and colophon
are trademarks of Simon & Schuster, Inc.

For information about special discounts for bulk purchases, please contact Simon & Schuster Special Sales at 1-866-506-1949 or business@simonandschuster.com.

The Simon & Schuster Speakers Bureau can bring authors to your live event. For more information or to book an event, contact the Simon & Schuster Speakers Bureau at 1-866-248-3049 or visit our website at www.simonspeakers.com.

Interior design by Oliver Munday

Manufactured in the United States of America

7 9 10 8 6

Library of Congress Cataloging-in-Publication Data

Names: Smith, Maggie, 1977– author.
Title: Keep moving : notes on loss, creativity, and change / Maggie Smith.
Description: New York : One Signal Publishers / Atria Books, 2020. |
Summary: "By Pushcart award-winning poet Maggie Smith, a collection of quotes and essays on facing life's challenges with creativity, courage, and resilience"—Provided by publisher.
Identifiers: LCCN 2019055475 (print) | LCCN 2019055476 (ebook) |
ISBN 9781982132071 (hardcover) | ISBN 9781982132088 (ebook)
Subjects: LCSH: Resilience (Personality trait)—Quotations. |
Creative Ability—Quotations. | Courage—Quotations.
Classification: LCC BF698.35.R47 S55 2020 (print) | LCC BF698.35.R47 (ebook) | DDC 155.2—dc23
LC record available at https://lccn.loc.gov/2019055475
LC ebook record available at https://lccn.loc.gov/2019055476

ISBN 978-1-9821-3207-1
ISBN 978-1-9821-3208-8 (ebook)

FOR YOU

CONTENTS

1. REVISION

The Long Book   2

Beauty Emergency   32

2. RESILIENCE

After the Fire   65

The Golden Repair   104

3. TRANSFORMATION

The Blue Rushes In   146

Nesters   183

Acknowledgments   214

1

REVISION

THE LONG BOOK

W hen my daughter was in second grade, she struggled with anxiety at bedtime—about death in particular, but also about the future in general. I would tuck her in at night and lie with her in the dark, holding her, listening.

"When will I die?" she'd ask. "Will you definitely die before me because you're older?"

What could I tell her? There are no guarantees in this life. But she was eight years old. I'd smooth her hair from her face and try my best to find the right words to calm her mind.

"Yes, I'm sure I'll die before you—but not until I'm very old, and you're a grown-up."

The questions kept coming: Will we miss each other when we're dead? Will we even know we're dead? When will it happen? Will we feel it?

"Life is long—a long book," I told her, "and you're only on the first chapter. Who wants to ruin a book by worrying about the end the whole time? Who wants to know how a book will end?"

"That would be boring," she said.

And of course, she was right.

Life is a book—long, if we're lucky—and we write it as we go. The ending isn't written, waiting for us to arrive. I'd known this all along, logically, but I hadn't yet felt it.

I thought that I knew my story.

I thought that what I was living was the whole story, but it was only a chapter.

After almost nineteen years together, my ex-husband and I separated. When my marriage ended—and with it the life I had known—the book did not end. Suddenly, there were so many blank pages, so many blank years ahead, to fill. There were days, weeks, when I could hardly get out of bed, hardly eat, but I felt the desire to write. If everything was going to fall apart, I told myself, at least I could create something. I was learning to live a different story, and I needed to find the words for it.

I struggled to write poems during this time. When I write a poem, I don't begin with an idea and then seek the language for it; I begin with language and follow where it leads me. But now I had ideas to work through, stories to tell, and I knew I would need a different kind of writing, a different container for my thoughts.

One morning, I wrote a goal for myself—just a couple of sentences—and posted it on social media. The next day, I wrote another one. Since then, I have written a note-to-self—an affirmation, an encouragement, a self-directive—every day.

The question I asked myself over and over in those first days and weeks was, "What now?" And that question inspired the last sentence of every goal: *Keep moving.* I had no idea what would happen next, what the next chapter would hold, but I had to get myself there.

The ending of one thing is also the beginning of another. What is the next adventure? There is room enough in this life—with its many endings, its many beginnings—for things you could not have imagined last week or last year or ten years ago.

KEEP MOVING.

Stop straining to hold the door to the past open, as if your old life is there, waiting, and you could just slip right in. Stop wasting your strength, because you can't go back. Muscle your way forward.

KEEP MOVING.

Write *breathe* on your to-do list. Write *blink*. Write *sit* and *eat*. Then cross everything off. How satisfying! Give yourself credit for living.

KEEP MOVING.

Remember putting on glasses for the first time: suddenly, the trees had individual leaves; the moon had defined edges. Try to see through that clear lens— everything as it is, not blurred or diffused by grief or anger. Look around you and marvel.

KEEP MOVING.

Stop calling your heart broken; your heart works just fine. If you are feeling—love, anger, gratitude, grief—it is because your heart is doing its work. Let it.

KEEP MOVING.

Focus on who you are
and what you've built,
not who you'd planned
on being and what you'd
expected to have. Trust
that the present moment—
however difficult, however
different from what you'd
imagined—has something
to teach you.

KEEP MOVING.

T o revise means, literally, "to look at again," to re-envision. Revision has always been my favorite part of writing. I know some writers love the rush of the new idea, the getting-it-down, the honeymoon period with a story or poem when it's still sparkling. But for me, the problem solving is what I love most: the challenge posed by the not-right words in the not-right order.

When I revise a piece of writing, I tend to whittle rather than expand as I go: the more time I spend with it, the smaller it gets, shrinking and shrinking as I try to be as concise as possible. (I joke that I could revise a poem to nothing—*poof!*—if I'm not careful.) What I'm doing is boiling the observation, the articulation, down—not being reductive, but reducing it to its most concentrated form. The final version will likely be small, but it will be potent.

As I work, I number the drafts—*one, two, three*—and if I get to *fifteen, sixteen, seventeen*, I know something's gone awry. Sometimes I put the draft aside for a day, a week, a month, or more, and I trust that Future Me will know better how to deal with it. Future Me will look at the poem, and something will click that didn't click before. Future Me will see the poem anew—see the section that isn't working, or see the potential in the piece that was not previously visible.

One thing I've learned about revision is that sometimes I need to go back in order to move forward. Sometimes I need to return to those earlier versions—*one, two, three*—to find the spark that drove me to the page in the first place. What can I excavate from those early versions? What necessary fire can I restore to the present iteration?

I believe in the importance of revision, but here's something I believe just as strongly: If you're not careful, you can revise the life right out of a piece of writing. If you're not careful, you can scrub all the weirdness and wildness right out of it. As counterintuitive as it sounds, you can polish it dull.

The same applies to our lives. If we're not careful, we can revise the life right out of them. We can polish our lives dull.

Revise the story
you tell yourself
about starting
over. Consider
not only how
terrifying change
can be but also
how exhilarating.
Consider this time
an opportunity
to make a new
and improved life.
KEEP MOVING.

Accept that while you crave resolution—an ending to the story, and a happy ending at that—this isn't how lives work. The arc you've learned doesn't apply, so stop trying to map the events of your life onto it. Just watch, listen, learn. KEEP MOVING.

Set down your grief for the life you intended to have but won't; the grief will be there when you're ready to come back to it. Now focus your mind on the life you intend to have. Commit to the present.

KEEP MOVING.

Stop watching and watching and watching the rearview mirror. Keep your eyes on the road. See the landscape scroll by like a filmstrip and don't miss a frame of it. **KEEP MOVING.**

Consider all you've outlived—including the life you thought you would have. You are durable, adaptable, resilient; just being here is a triumph. Hour by hour, prove the voice inside wrong—the one that says you can't do it. Do it.

KEEP MOVING.

You need today because there is more—because yesterday was not enough. Believe there is more to see and feel and do—and try your best to see it, feel it, do it.

KEEP MOVING.

W hen I think about revising my life, I think about learning to see it anew, and to see in it possibilities I could not see before.

For almost all of my adult life to this point, I'd told my story in first-person plural: *we*. Now the *we* is an *I*. Now the only plural is possessive: *our* children. (And yet, of course, the children are not *ours*. We do not own the children any more than we own each other—which is to say, not at all.) But I know one thing for certain: our stories belong to us. I'm the protagonist in my own life, or damn well should be, and you're the protagonist in yours. Whether you're on the first draft of your life or the second or the tenth, it's yours to keep writing—in all of its messiness and fragility and terror and beauty.

I began writing a goal for myself each day, even when I was struggling and optimism felt less than natural. What kept me going was the idea that hope begets hope, and that practicing hope and courage on a daily basis might help me arrive at that better place.

Yes, there is an element of *fake it until you make it* to being hopeful in a time of crisis. But why not? Perhaps when we try hope on for size, it may not fit at first—it may hang on us, several sizes too big—but if we keep wearing it, we will grow into it.

I find now that hope fits better than it did a year ago. It's fitting better all the time. I'm growing into that garment, and it's becoming a second skin. This is a kind of revision.

What do you do *religiously*—
not only often, but with
great love and faith?
Writing, painting, running,
volunteering? Do one
of those things today; do
something religiously.

KEEP MOVING.

What you deserve is not pain but peace—peace in whatever form it takes. If your peace is small and broken, carry it close to you, whisper to it now and then, nurture it until it grows and can take a turn carrying you.

KEEP MOVING.

Think about geologic time: how the slightest shifts, imperceptible daily, carve canyons and make mountains. Trust that you are making progress even if you can't yet see it. **KEEP MOVING.**

Accept that you are
a work in progress,
both a revision and
a draft: you are
better and more
complete than
earlier versions of
yourself, but you
also have work
to do. Be open
to change. Allow
yourself to be
revised.

KEEP MOVING.

All you need to do today is live the best you can. Even if in this difficult time your best doesn't feel like enough, it is enough. And trust that your best tomorrow will be even better than today's: that is healing.

KEEP MOVING.

Imagine what might await you on the other side of this dark forest. Imagine the clearing, the sunshine.

KEEP MOVING.

F aced with so many blank pages—all the blank days, months, and years ahead—I am learning to write this next draft in first-person singular. I am revising my *thinking* about loss. Part of the work is asking myself difficult questions:

Who did you want to be, before?
What did you sacrifice, compromise, or leave behind along the way?
What of that earlier draft of yourself can you salvage?
What spark can you find?
How can you pull that spark into your present life? The story you are living now?

Our lives may not unfold the way we'd hoped or expected, but the alternative—flipping to the end of the book, knowing the ending before we get there—is not only impossible but joyless. Polished dull. As my daughter said, in her eight-year-old wisdom, "That would be boring."

Revising our stories—our lives—is no easy task. Our stories may take strange turns. We may find that we are living part mystery, part romance, part comedy, part tragedy, part ghost story. We don't know what will happen next or how it will end. But we keep moving.

Hope is imaginative:
it allows you to
envision what might
be up ahead, even
when you see nothing.
Hope. Imagine your
way forward.

KEEP MOVING.

Stop expecting the worst: at least as many things could go right as could go wrong. Think of optimism as a way of sitting in the sun now, regardless of what the weather might be tomorrow or next week.

KEEP MOVING.

Maybe you have a little voice inside that says you aren't strong enough to handle what life's left at your feet. That voice lies. Prove it wrong today—then repeat, repeat, repeat.

KEEP MOVING.

Prepare to be uncomfortable in service of transformation. If you want to thrive in a new life, you're going to have to change, too. It may feel like you're breathing different air, but trust that you can adapt. Press on.

KEEP MOVING.

Accept that you
may have to
break on the way
to wholeness, as
counterintuitive
as that sounds.
Think of it as
a reassembling.
You will not
be the same,
you will not be
unscarred, but
you will be better
than before.
KEEP MOVING.

Stop thinking of change as interruption to a story; the story was always going to change, many times. It was never guaranteed. In fact, only change is guaranteed. Expect it today, and from now on.

KEEP MOVING.

BEAUTY EMERGENCY

O ne morning I looked out the bathroom window and couldn't believe the sky I saw—banded magenta, aqua, purple. I shouted to the kids, "Hurry, look out back!"

My son, who was downstairs, went straight to the back door to see the sunrise. But my daughter came running into the upstairs bathroom. "What's wrong?" she asked.

"Nothing's wrong—just a beauty emergency. Look at that sky!" Because she is my child, she knows what a beauty emergency is: one of those things you have to look at now, before it's gone.

Sure enough, I looked out the window just a few minutes later and the sky was back to normal, as if that magic painting had never been made. But we'd seen it. We knew that the beauty had happened.

When my ex-husband moved out of our house, it was late fall. That seemed fitting. The air smelled of smoke, and all the green trees were rusting. I remember walking home from the elementary school one morning after dropping off the kids, looking at the leaves—red, orange, yellow, a purple almost black—and letting it sink in: *All this color came from decay.*

I was reminded of a song recorded by the Byrds, originally written by Pete Seeger—"Turn! Turn! Turn!" Almost all of the lyrics were pulled verbatim from Ecclesiastes: "To everything there is a season." But the "turn, turn, turn" was all Seeger.

The idea is a familiar one, whether you first learned it from the Bible or from the radio: Everything has its time. There is a time for decay and a time for growth. The trick is that we don't get to change the season;

we can't skip ahead to healing because we're tired of grieving, or because it's taking too long.

I pictured myself letting one bright leaf fall. Then another, and another. I imagined those fallen leaves crisping in the yards, filling up the gutters. I imagined raking them into piles and letting the kids jump in them. The image helped me through that season, day by day, leaf by leaf. Turn, turn, turn.

Changing one
thing can change
everything.
Let more light
into your life
by letting more
light into this
day. Then repeat,
repeat, repeat.
KEEP MOVING.

Apprentice yourself
to the present.
Apprentice yourself
to right now.
Let it teach you.
Listen to it and
watch it.
Trust it to show you
how to stay inside it
even as time passes.
KEEP MOVING.

Stop rewinding and replaying the past in your mind. Live here, now. Give the present the gift of your full attention.

KEEP MOVING.

Trust that everything will be okay, but that doesn't mean that everything will be restored. Start making yourself at home in your life as it is. Look around and look ahead.

KEEP MOVING.

You are not betraying your grief by feeling joy. You are not being graded, and you do not receive extra credit for being miserable 100% of the time. Find pockets of relief, even happiness, when and where you can.

KEEP MOVING.

Even though
so much seems
to be in pieces,
trust your own
wholeness.
Accept that you
cannot be sure
of everything,
but be sure of
yourself.

KEEP MOVING.

T hat fall my ex-husband and I had decided to work toward a dissolution. Now when I read or hear someone say the word *dissolve*, I see my marriage as a tablet at the bottom of a glass, obscured by a riot of bubbles. It was less than it was, and then less, and then less. And now it is gone—or still there but invisible. It colors the water in the glass.

If you look up *dissolution*, you will find the technical definition: "the action or process of dissolving or being dissolved." You will find synonyms that suggest a vanishing, a falling apart: *dissolving, liquefaction, melting, disintegration, decomposition, breaking up*. And you will certainly learn more than you wanted to know about chemistry, about molecules, about solvents and solutes. You will also find the formal definition: "death."

It does feel like a death—the fizzing away of so much I'd thought was solid, ineffable.

The magic was gone, the sky flat gray, the trees bare. It seemed strange to me that the sun arrived and departed each day as if nothing had happened. It was too easy to believe that our life had never been beautiful, that we had never been happy. But it had been a beautiful life, a beautiful season. I remember.

That year fall came and went, winter came and went. A new year began, and spring showed up right on time, scattering its wild violets across the lawn and tricking the daffodils and magnolias into opening too early. The present seemed to be chiding me—*I'm not waiting for you. Come along now.* I knew I couldn't stay behind. The past isn't a place we can live. It dissolves behind us.

It was in those lush green months of spring—beauty emergencies everywhere—that the grief started to recede, bit by bit. I began to imagine a new life for myself—I didn't know what it would look like, but I finally believed it was possible. It was spring in the world, and I had to learn to trust that I was being made new in ways I couldn't yet see. I imagined the seeds and bulbs sleeping in the dirt, waiting for their turn in the light and the air.

Trust that you have
the materials you
need in order to
build and to make
necessary changes to
your life: courage,
intelligence, empathy,
imagination. Believe
that you are capable
and ready. Get to
work in some small
way today.

KEEP MOVING.

Everything is temporary. You can't keep a white-knuckled hold on what you love or on what has hurt you. Loosen your grip on your grief today, if only a bit.

KEEP MOVING.

For every worry or hurt that chews at your mind, think of one thing you're grateful for, however small. One by one, fill your mind with them. Let them crowd out the worry and the hurt.

KEEP MOVING.

Do not ignore
what hurts.
Even as you feel
yourself beginning
to heal, the wound
may be with you
indefinitely, like
a phantom limb.
That ghost is a
teacher; learn
from it all you can.

KEEP MOVING.

Whatever is gone, you've outlasted it. Grieve the "withoutness" but celebrate surviving it, outliving it. Be here.

KEEP MOVING.

Be sure of at least one thing in this moment—that you are loved and worthy of love. Hold tightly to what you know to be real and true and good about who you are. Be sure of yourself.

KEEP MOVING.

M ourning a living person is different from mourning the dead. A woman whose husband dies is a widow. But there is no word for a person who grieves a living person—a child, a partner, an estranged family member or dear friend. There is no name for what you are when a part of your life and identity dies, but you go on living. There is no name for what you are when you outlive the life you expected to have and find yourself in a kind of afterlife.

When my mother's mother died, I remember a feeling of erosion—dissolving. She'd already been diagnosed with Alzheimer's when my ex-husband and I met, but then the news got worse: cancer. She didn't live to see our engagement or our wedding. She didn't get to hear our vows, which we'd written on the porch of a half double we rented on Arcadia Avenue. I remember one in particular: *I will love your family as my own.*

My grandmother has been gone as many years as my ex-husband and I were together. Soon she will have been gone twenty years, longer than I was married. Her death will keep growing in this way, longer and longer, but there will be two dates for our marriage, as if on a headstone: the day it began, and the day it ended.

Rhett, my second child, was born on October 18, 2012, twelve years to the day after my grandmother died. It is not coincidence; I scheduled the Caesarean for that morning. In my family, October 18 is a day of color—red, orange, yellow, a purple almost black—and a day of decay. A birthday and a death day.

Accept that sometimes dismantling has to happen before you can build. As you look at the mess of life's pieces and parts around you, trust that the materials you need are there. Start sorting: Which can go? Which should stay? How will you use them? Start now.

KEEP MOVING.

Instead of
struggling at
every roadblock,
make a new way
entirely. Keep an
open mind: even
the destination
may change.

KEEP MOVING.

Get back up. Dust yourself off. Remember that you're playing the long game, and trust that over time, the good days will outnumber the bad. Do what you can to make this day more livable than yesterday. **KEEP MOVING.**

You can't go back. You have no choice but to go forward, but you can choose how you get there. Walk, don't crawl, toward your new life—your next life. Carry yourself with as much courage as you can muster.

KEEP MOVING.

Don't wait for your life to magically come together—it's your work to do. Every day, every moment, you are making your life from scratch. Today, take one step, however small, toward creating a life you can be proud of.

KEEP MOVING.

Keep in mind that grief does not get better day by day in some predictable way. Time doesn't take another stone off the pile each day until the pile is gone. Be patient. Expect the unexpected.

KEEP MOVING.

W hen the present nudges me, *Come along now,* I write as a way of coming along. I write as a way of creating spring regardless of the heart's—or world's—season. I try to approach each page, each day, with the excitement of a beginner. My children inspire so many of my poems precisely because they are beginners in the world, curious and excited about what they experience. When we take walks together, they snap me back into the moment: *Mom, look! Hurry, look!*

I look, and I look *now,* because I might miss the seed pod twirling down, or the squirrels chasing each other through the treetops, or a kind of wildflower that looks like a lion's face. What's more, I might miss the fleeting look of wonder on my children's faces.

I might miss the season I'm in.

Each season has its gifts. What did my life's hardest season give to me? Most of all, belief in my own ability not only to come back after a long winter but to grow stronger, more alive. Belief that change makes everything possible. Belief in my own spring. In the meantime, thanks to the bare trees, I can see more sky. It's a beauty emergency—all that blue through the branches.

Do not let loss drain the color from everything. Open your eyes to the brilliance around you: it's still here.

KEEP MOVING.

You can think about the past, casting your mind back, or think about the future, casting your mind forward, but you live here, in the present. Keep your mind here the best you can today.

KEEP MOVING.

Throw away
what you think
you know.
Throw away the
old blueprint for
something that
will not be built.
Instead, rethink
that space.
Now it can be
anything: What
will it be?

KEEP MOVING.

MAGGIE SMITH

Close the gap between yourself and your spirit—the person you know you can be. Let your choices reflect the person you want to become, not just the person you think you are.

KEEP MOVING.

Accept that what's chasing you isn't going to stop or give up. You're going to have to turn and face it. Plant your feet. Chin up. Stare it down, then keep going.

KEEP MOVING.

Approach today—each day—
with eagerness. Approach
the day with the spirit of
Yes, please. Drink it in.
Yes, please. More, please.

KEEP MOVING.

2—

RESILIENCE

AFTER THE FIRE

O ne of my favorite words is *serotinous*. The word sounds much sexier than its definition: "remaining closed on the tree with seed dissemination delayed or occurring gradually." Serotinous pinecones are thick and strong, glued shut for years by a coating of resin. In order to open, the cones need fire—flames hot enough to melt the resin and release the seeds, which fall to the forest floor or are carried away to become new trees.

I am not a dendrologist or any kind of *-ist*. I have never worked as a park ranger or a firefighter. No, I learned the word *serotinous* because I'm a mother who watches nature documentaries with her children—children who, even at their young ages, greatly prefer the distinguished voice of David Attenborough to other narrators. One afternoon we sat together on the couch and watched a film about the landscape and wildlife of the American West. I was transfixed as fire swept through the trees like a bright wind.

And the cones of the lodgepole pine, having waited for so long for fire's touch, opened.

It is not your job to make
other people comfortable
with who you are. Be wary
of those who don't want
you to change or grow.
Grow anyway—
there is no alternative.

KEEP MOVING.

Do not be led by fear;
fear cannot lead you out
of the dark. Find whatever
bits of hope you can—
a trail of even the smallest
bread crumbs, even the
tiniest pebbles reflecting the
moonlight—and follow them.

KEEP MOVING.

Let life be a little ramshackle right now. Let it be messy and jerry-rigged and held together with binder clips and duct tape. Let it not be okay—and know, for now, that's okay.

KEEP MOVING.

When life held
your hand in the
flames, it taught
you something
about the kind
of burning you
can endure. You
survived: don't
forget that, and
don't diminish it.

KEEP MOVING.

Be thankful for your wounds, as strange as that sounds; the ways you've been hurt and the ways you've faltered make you useful to other people. Empathy is a kind of fellowship; be thankful that your wounds made this togetherness possible.

KEEP MOVING.

Fight the urge to withdraw,
to fold in on yourself, as if
your pain is contagious and
might infect someone else.
We are here to take care
of one another; the care is
what's catching, spreading
person to person to person.
So take—and give—care.

KEEP MOVING.

A s anyone in my family will tell you, I was not a brave child. I was afraid of heights, afraid of the dark, but also afraid of saying the wrong things, wearing the wrong things, liking the wrong things. I wasn't a "joiner." I didn't want to do anything unless I was guaranteed to succeed.

I was the child who refused to ride the roller coasters at the amusement park, so I spent time each summer sitting on a bench with a small box of saltwater taffy, waiting for my sisters and parents to return breathless from rides called the Demon Drop and the Corkscrew and the Magnum. I would ride a few small rides—the Spider, the Scrambler. One was called the Troika. It was one of those many-armed spinning rides that never got too high off the ground. I loved it.

My parents joked that my younger sisters would be willing to ride the Magnum, the tallest and steepest coaster in the state at the time, after dark. They weren't afraid.

But me? I remember one of them saying, "Maggie would ride the Troika . . . at dusk."

It's still a running joke in my family—"the Troika at dusk"—a phrase that's shorthand for the kind of kid I was. "The Troika at Dusk" would be a good slogan for my level of courage not only throughout my childhood but well into adulthood.

Even in my twenties, I dreaded ordering a pizza or making dinner reservations over the phone. I dreaded depositing a check at the bank or picking up meds at the pharmacy. I would find any excuse not to talk to strangers, often counting on my then boyfriend—now ex-husband—to handle interactions with the landlord, the plumber, the cable company. I was so nervous to ride a city bus for the first time, in graduate school, that he took me on a dry run. I remember following him up the steps once the bus doors opened, and being shown how to feed my money in and take a ticket. We sat down near the back, and he pointed out the yellow cable to pull when my stop was approaching.

For most of my life, I hated surprises. My mother says that even in preschool, I refused to get into the car unless she told me where we were going. She'd have to whisper the location to me so as not to ruin the surprise for my sisters. I thought of change as some interruption in my life, a veering off course, and so when life's fires swept through, I felt not only grief but terror. I had to stand and watch life as I knew it burn down, and hope that something could be salvaged.

Tell yourself kinder truths. You are not failing at life; you are reeling, sure, but you are succeeding at surviving.

KEEP MOVING.

All you have to do today is live the best you can. Even if your best doesn't feel like much right now, your best will get better and better. Trust that someday you will look back and realize you survived, one day at a time.

KEEP MOVING.

Praise the roots of the plant—what grounds it and allows it to grow—not only the flower. Without quiet, unseen work happening in the dark, nothing would open in the light. Thrive and be grateful you can.

KEEP MOVING.

Forget what you've learned about scarcity; it doesn't apply to intangibles. When someone triumphs or finds joy, they aren't taking what would have been yours— they are making more of what we all draw from. There is more than enough.

KEEP MOVING.

There is a fine
line between
self-protection
and self-sabotage.
Do not withhold
love from others
just because someone
withheld it from you.
Be generous.
In some way today,
give of your heart and
your time.

KEEP MOVING.

Prioritize your own happiness, security, and wellness. You cannot care for anyone else until and unless you care for yourself. Secure your own mask first.

KEEP MOVING.

M ercifully, when an actual fire approaches—wild and ravenous, baring its teeth—the forest doesn't fear. The trees don't brace themselves against the searing heat or blame themselves for being in its path. But when we find ourselves in another kind of fire, too often we feel shame. The voice inside says, *If you'd deserved the good things, you would have gotten them.* The voice says, *You must be a monster if someone is willing to put themselves and their family through hell to get away from you.* It says, *You should have known better, should have seen this coming.* It says, *You deserved this. You are unworthy of love, happiness, success.*

But that voice lies. That voice is a fire all its own.

I remember driving my son home from preschool one afternoon when he was around four years old. I'd asked him how his day went, and he'd said something about feeling "embarrassed" because of something that had happened that day. My initial instinct was, *Is that what he means?* So I asked him—a test—"What does *embarrassed* mean?"

"It means *scared*," he said.

I had to sit with that for a minute, turning from the main road into our neighborhood, because yes, of course, he was right. What is embarrassment but a relative of fear? You've been seen—caught—at being imperfect. My four-year-old son taught me something about fear that day. And when someone teaches you something about fear, they are also teaching you something about courage.

Spend time with—or talk to—someone who loves you exactly as you are. See yourself through their eyes. From this day on, commit to becoming someone who loves you exactly as you are.

KEEP MOVING.

Every person you encounter
has a struggle, a hidden
wound, something they carry
that hurts them. Be kind—
maybe something you do or
say today will be the good
medicine they need.

KEEP MOVING.

Do not stop
at the wall
looming
before you.
Make a door.
Make a door
wide enough
not only for you
but for others.

KEEP MOVING.

Ask yourself about the kind of life you want: What would you do day to day, and with whom, and where? Consider the life you have. Do one thing today, however small, to close the gap between the two.

KEEP MOVING.

Be brave enough to ask
for help when you need it.
There is no merit badge for
Doing All the Hard Things
Alone. Reach out.

KEEP MOVING.

It is not enough to "think positive"; you have to "do positive." Push hope from theory into practice. Do something today, however small, to light up your own life. Or shine on someone else— the light will reach you, too.

KEEP MOVING.

W hen I think about the child I was—afraid of change, afraid of even the possibility of failure—I want to mother her. I want to convince her to try and to keep trying, regardless of the outcome. When I think about the young woman I was—still so timid and insecure, unhappy despite her beautiful life—I want to go back, grab her by the shoulders, and shake her awake.

When a forest burns, the trees have no choice but to stand and endure the burning. Unlike jackrabbits or deer or hawks, they can't run or fly away. But some trees have adapted not only to survive but to thrive in fire: the lodgepole pine, the jack pine, the Table Mountain pine. These trees require fire. They are stronger and greater in number for having spent time in the flames.

I have no idea what the next twenty years of my life will look like, only that they won't—*can't*—look like the last twenty years. That forest has burned. And yet. And yet! I am still here.

> it is not unusual to sift
> through ashes
> and find an unburnt picture

—NIKKI GIOVANNI

Think of grief,
anger, worry as
bricks or planks of
wood. Stop staring
at the materials, half
believing they were
delivered to you by
mistake, half expecting
a truck to haul
them away. Accept
that these are your
materials right now.
Start building.

KEEP MOVING.

Everything has been said and felt and done before—but not by you. You are the only one who can make your art, who can love in your unique way. So do it.

KEEP MOVING.

Maybe you don't
know what kind of
work you should be
doing in the world.
Maybe you think
everyone else has it
figured out.
(They don't.)
Your work is being
yourself, offering what
you can to others.
You've been doing it
all along. Now do it
with intention.
KEEP MOVING.

Think of the moon, how
solitary it looks, and
know that's just a trick of
perspective: the moon is
not alone, and neither are
you. Remember how vast
and star-filled your universe
is, and how it continues to
expand. Shine on.

KEEP MOVING.

Love is not
something you
earn. Love is a
gift economy,
like poetry.
Give it away
and receive
it graciously.
Move on from
those who
withhold it.

KEEP MOVING.

Accept that you do not get to choose who loves you, who keeps their promises, who forgives. But you can choose to love, to keep your promises, to forgive. Choose well. Have—and live—your own say.

KEEP MOVING.

n my life I have stood through fires as a fearful person, a person to whom courage does not come easily, and I've learned from what I was up against. Yes, each fire has been a teacher. Each fire teaches us what we can endure. Each fire teaches us about resilience and renewal—that something will grow after it passes, and that what grows after a fire could not have been born any other way.

Post-traumatic stress is a familiar idea. We have come to accept, if not expect, that trauma results in psychological and physical damage. But what about post-traumatic growth, "the positive change experienced as a result of the struggle with a major life crisis or a traumatic event"? Researchers have found that humans not only "bounce back" after traumatic events but actually push forward—taking professional risks, strengthening their relationships, and feeling a deeper sense of gratitude.

So often we think of loss as only destructive, but it is also generative—because every ending is also a beginning. When one thing vanishes, a space is created in its place. Of course, when we grieve, we are mourning a loss, but why not also ask what might grow in that barren place? Why not ask: What could I plant there?

Serotinous is a word I cherish because it reminds me of what is made possible by disaster, what fire gives even as it takes.

I wish I could go back and tell the fearful young person I was what I know now about fire and growth. What would I say to her? Even if you do not feel brave, practice bravery. There will be times in your life when you feel as if life is burning down around you, but know that renewal is in its wake. Trust in what will open, what will grow, after something else has burned away, even when the landscape is charred black. And trust that one of the things guaranteed to grow—time after time, fire after fire—is you. Possibilities, like seeds, are being released into the air.

Consider that
your ideas about
happiness—what
you think it should
look like, feel like,
entail, provide—
might be hindering
your experience
of it. Set aside your
expectations. Watch,
listen, learn, feel.

KEEP MOVING.

Think hard about
independence—and
the illusion of it. Take one
action, however small,
to disentangle yourself from
a person or situation
that holds you down
or holds you back. Then
take one action to help
someone else do the same.

KEEP MOVING.

Focus on living rather than only living through or living with; rather than gutting it out, hanging in there, coping, withstanding. Think of *living* as bigger and more than surviving.

KEEP MOVING.

Believe there is peace up ahead, even if there's no sign of it on the horizon. Even if you can't see it yet, trust it's there. In the meantime, do what you can to bring a little peace to this day. Breathe.

KEEP MOVING.

Even if you don't believe you have "a purpose," think about the work you can do in the world that would make a difference to others. What art can you make, what comfort can you bring, what wrong can you set right? If you can do it, you should do it. KEEP MOVING.

MAGGIE SMITH

Accept that what hurt yesterday is going to hurt today and tomorrow. It might always hurt—but not like this. The pain may be slowing you down now, but trust that in time you will learn to move with it, because you are strong enough.

KEEP MOVING.

Maybe we say "holding a grudge" because that kind of resentment is a heavy thing you have to wrap your arms around to carry. Holding it weighs you down, not the other person. Set it down anytime. Right now, for instance.

KEEP MOVING.

Stop waiting
on some grand
permission to
change your life.
The universe is
not going to tell
you it's okay.
Tell yourself
it's okay.

KEEP MOVING.

THE GOLDEN REPAIR

T he word *kintsugi*, which translates as "golden joinery" (or *kintsukuroi*, "golden repair"), refers to the centuries-old Japanese art of mending broken ceramics with gold. The artists don't hide the cracks in the bowl—they fill them with lacquer dusted with powdered gold, silver, or platinum, so that its seams gleam where it was pieced back together.

Kintsugi is related to the Japanese philosophy of *wabi-sabi*, which celebrates imperfection and impermanence, as well as *mushin*, the acceptance of change. The artist honors the object's history—what it went through to become what it is now—and gives it new life. The brokenness is not only the most beautiful part but also the strongest part.

When I think about healing after loss or trauma, I think of pottery made whole again with gold.

Do not turn away joy—
even if it arrives at an
inconvenient time, even
if you think you should
be grieving, even if you
think it's "too soon."
Joy is always on time.

KEEP MOVING.

Recognize the
difference between
the end and *an* end.
Articles matter. Try
not to catastrophize.
For as short as life
is, know it is also a
container big enough
to hold things you
could not have
imagined six months
ago or six years ago.

KEEP MOVING.

Do not give up on yourself, even if someone gave up on you. Choose yourself. Do something today, however small, to invest in your own happiness.

KEEP MOVING.

What you call *luck* is only possible if you've laid its foundation yourself. Do something today, however small, to prepare for luck, to put yourself in luck's way. Then repeat, repeat, repeat.

KEEP MOVING.

Stop searching yourself, trying
to understand why someone else
treated you the way they did: the
answer is not inside you, it's inside
them, out of reach. Instead,
work on understanding—
truly knowing—yourself.

KEEP MOVING.

Reflect on what you've lived through—and look, you're still here. Look back at the road you've traveled to get to this place, and know you've built the strength to travel the next stretch—and the next one, and the next.

KEEP MOVING.

If you are being
gentle with yourself
during a difficult
time, that is
not self-pity.
You would show
compassion to
a friend in pain,
even a stranger,
so why withhold it
from yourself?
Don't.

KEEP MOVING.

Think about the word *spell*—meaning "a state of enchantment" or "a brief period of time." When a chapter of your life ends, you may feel that a spell has been broken; you may feel disenchanted, but new magic is coming. Better yet: make new magic.

KEEP MOVING.

Consider what you've
learned about yourself
through grief: Now
you know how strong
you are. Now you
know what you can
bear. Think about this
strange gift—being
confident in what you
are capable of.
Go forward with
that strength.

KEEP MOVING.

W hen my daughter, Violet, was born in December 2008, motherhood was not what I'd seen in movies. She rarely slept, and only when held. She cried insistently, refusing comfort. Desperate for lullabies, I sang her "Graceland" and "Lucy in the Sky with Diamonds," because, even exhausted, I knew the words. I sang her "You Are My Sunshine," as if singing it could make it so. I played the white noise CD on a loop. I bounced, jiggled, walked, drove. I cried in the shower, when I could steal away to take one.

I said to my then husband, "She doesn't love me, she only wants me for food." I said, "Why did we do this?" We'd had a good life. We'd ruined our good life. We'd done this to ourselves.

I returned to work two weeks earlier than planned—mostly to escape, to row away from the lonely island we lived on together. I remember dropping her off at day care. I remember her sitting in a baby swing in a ladybug outfit, clutching a little burp cloth like a security blanket, her eyes focusing on something across the room. I left her there. I cried, but I was free.

And my dread, which I never treated, which I never even called by its proper name, began to dissolve. I could almost taste it—a hard lozenge dissolving in the heat of my mouth.

Do not talk down to yourself for struggling; the struggle is part of the transformation. Trust that the version of yourself that emerges on the other side will be stronger for it.

KEEP MOVING.

Stop focusing on what is behind you. It's growing smaller and smaller, miniaturizing in the distance; stop squinting at it, as if it has answers. Today, keep your eyes on where you are going, not where you have been. **KEEP MOVING.**

Let the hard days be hard. When you mourn a person, it's a form of love. You mourn their loss because they mattered, because the world without them is diminished. Sit still with your grief if you need to, then lift it and carry it with you.

KEEP MOVING.

Take stock of
what you can see
in your life now
that parts of it are
gone: What view
has that space
created? What
can you see now
that you couldn't
before? Take in
the new view.
KEEP MOVING.

Let change—even traumatic upheaval—remind you that anything is possible. When the dark cloud of chaos hangs over you, let possibility be the silver lining.

KEEP MOVING.

Ask yourself what part of you is holding on to pain because it is familiar, because letting go would require you to do something different, to fill that space. And what could fill that space? Today, loosen your grip on the pain. Let it go, bit by bit.

KEEP MOVING.

t took us years to decide to have another child. I was terrified of regretting it, terrified of those bathrobe days, bathrobe weeks. Terrified of the faraway look I'd seen in photographs of myself, that hollow, scraped-out feeling.

What I didn't expect was that the road would be so difficult once we finally decided to travel it. I miscarried twice in 2011, once at home and once, to my horror, in the restroom at work. I felt broken. I thought of my body as a broken thing.

The year of the miscarriages was also the year of obsession. I insisted on test after test. I charted. I listed. If this, then that. If my levels are X, then we can try Y again. We did decide to try again one last time in 2012. On Valentine's Day, the day after my thirty-fifth birthday, I told my then husband I was pregnant. "Here we go again," he said. We both expected the worst.

But weeks later, there it was on the fuzzy gray screen: a small flicker. Still, the bargaining, the obsessive worry, the guardedness did not resolve. I didn't talk or write about the miscarriages because I was ashamed of my body's brokenness, but I was also superstitious. I didn't want to somehow jinx our last chance at another child. We'd agreed we would not try again.

Twice there was almost a child, as if *almost* were a variety of child, like an apple—Suncrisp, Red Delicious, Rome, Almost. And I was some variety of widow, some variety of orphan, some terrible hybrid: there is no name for a mother of almost a child. I'd seen my medical chart. *Pregnancies: 4. Live births: 1.* For nine months, I expected blood.

Fight the urge to
withdraw when you're
in pain—to make
yourself small, to
secret yourself away,
as if to avoid inflicting
yourself on others.
We are here to take
care of one another,
so let the people who
love you do their
work. It will be your
turn soon enough.

KEEP MOVING.

Your life is your
own, and your
work is your
own, and those
things can be
anything you
want them to be.
It's up to you.

KEEP MOVING.

Let this be a time of
reclamation. Today, reclaim
a space, a song, an object,
a memory that has brought
you pain. Make it new.

KEEP MOVING.

Expect that what you tend to will grow. Expect that what you feed with your care and attention, what you shine your light on, will thrive. Choose wisely.

KEEP MOVING.

Vulnerability is strength. Do not compound your pain by being ashamed of it. Be vulnerable. Be strong.

KEEP MOVING.

Imagine the view from
an airplane window:
everything toy-sized,
miniaturized below.
Whatever feels enormous
now won't always be this
size. You'll rise up and
away from it.

KEEP MOVING.

O ur son was born in October. He looked like an Elvis impersonator—almost ten pounds, with a full head of dark hair and sideburns. He was the child who almost wasn't. If I'd believed in miracles, he would have been one. He was the sun, the light at the end of a long darkness.

At first, he was so calm and quiet, I thought the curse had been broken. But after a couple of weeks, he emerged from the fog of birth. Colic. Acid reflux. Dairy sensitivity. Extreme wakefulness. By December, I found myself at the edge again, but this time with a four-year-old to care for. My mind's engine ran and ran until it smoked. I wrote everything down. I couldn't sleep. I worried about what the next day would bring. I worried about being left alone with him. I dreaded morning. I berated myself: *Why isn't my gratitude for him enough to keep me happy? Why did I willingly maroon myself on an island with a newborn a second time? Why did I think it would be different? Why isn't it different?*

I resented my then husband for having an office to go off to each day. And when I snapped at him, when I stomped around the kitchen, slamming the cabinet doors, he said: "You chose this. This is what you wanted."

What he meant was: *You knew I'd be at work and you'd be at home. You knew it would be hard.*

What I heard was: *I told you so.*

They call the first three months of a baby's life "the fourth trimester." Horses can practically run out of the womb. Even a deer can stand, sticky, and walk. But human infants are helpless, blind, bawling, not ready to be in the world—and I wasn't ready, either. I wasn't ready for this.

Looking back, I can't help but think that I compounded my pain by being ashamed of it, trying to hide it. What's worse than suffering? Suffering but pretending that you aren't—by gluing ourselves, our lives, back together, hoping no one notices the many breaks.

I know now that miscarriage is a predictor for postpartum depression. Of course it is. I'd been pregnant three times in two years. My hormones had been all over the place, and I'd been heartbroken, wrung out, exhausted, and scared. My chart was updated. *Pregnancies: 4. Live births: 2.* I was lucky—*am* lucky—to have two healthy children, but there is no name for a mother with only half of her children living in this world. I didn't know how to talk or write about it.

Trust that as fast and far as your fear can travel, your courage will outrun it. Focus on a point in the distance. Imagine a tether of light pulling you toward it, widening the distance between you and whatever would snap at your heels. Eyes ahead.

KEEP MOVING.

Being strong,
bracing yourself
against hurt, can
get in the way of
actual healing—
the real work.
Open up today,
if only a little.
Crack the window
and let in the
light and the air.

KEEP MOVING.

Feel without judging
yourself for the
feeling. Whatever it
is—disappointment
or surprise, sadness
or joy, envy or
contentment, fear
or relief—sit with
it and in it. Then
let it go on its way,
making room for
what will arrive
in its wake.

KEEP MOVING.

Remember a time when you forgave someone, how freeing that felt. You deserve your mercy as much as anyone else does. Forgive yourself for something today, something you wish you'd done differently. Just let it go. Free yourself from it.

KEEP MOVING.

Do not be
ashamed of the
intensity of your
emotion. That's
your humanity.
Grief can be feral,
wild, frightening.
Give it a safe
place to live.

KEEP MOVING.

Diamonds are created
from intense pressure
over long periods of
time; pearls are formed
around irritants.
Precious things are
made from discomfort.
KEEP MOVING.

T he idea behind *Kintsugi* is that a thing is beautiful not in spite of the damage it suffered but *because* of the damage. I had to learn to forgive myself for my brokenness and to be honest about what I was going through. As I talk and write candidly about my miscarriages, my struggles with postpartum depression and anxiety, and my divorce, I feel myself filling the cracks with gold. I am letting the seams show— those signs of survival, those scars I can be proud of—and letting them shine.

Writing about my own loss and grief has given me a sense of purpose and a new appreciation of, even gratitude for, my wounds. Of course, the scales are not balanced. I would choose a happy, intact family over any words I'll write about the loss of that happy, intact family. I would choose live births every time. But I wasn't given that choice. If I experience brokenness, the least I can do is make something from it, something that might help me heal.

I consider the literary community my chosen family. Who reached out to me when my marriage ended? Writers, artists, musicians—a wild, generous bunch. Some of them I knew in person, and some I knew only on social media. Regardless, they called and wrote. They sent books, paintings, postcards, records. They sent flowers and cards and crystals and essential oils. They offered me time at writing retreats or guest rooms to crash in if I needed to get away. They sent messages of encouragement. They checked in.

Poetry—and writing in general—is a solitary vocation. But I have never felt alone in it. I am not alone in it now. Look, you're here, too.

Our struggles will transform us eventually, if we let them. And they may transform other people, too, if we let the breaks show—only if we honor imperfection and impermanence, filling the cracks with gold, can we be mirrors for each other. What we say when we write about our own brokenness is not *Look at me* but *Look at us*.

Commit yourself to the present. Loosen your grip on the life you had before—before a loss, an upheaval, a change that called everything into question—so that you can be here, where you're needed, right now.

KEEP MOVING.

Do something today that will bring you joy even if you know you will not do it well. Let go of the idea that you have to be the best at something to do it. Train yourself to crave experience, not perfection.

KEEP MOVING.

Do not wait for someone else to rescue you. Do one thing today, however small, in Operation: Save Yourself. Make a ladder, pick a lock. KEEP MOVING.

Stop rattling
around inside
yourself, as if
you are small;
you are not
small. Celebrate
the ways you
have grown
and changed.
Fill yourself
to the skin.
KEEP MOVING.

Do not allow someone else's choices to ruin your waking hours or interrupt your sleep. The only words and actions you can control are your own, so focus on your own integrity, generosity, honesty. Rise above.

KEEP MOVING.

Know yourself by your
actions. You are not what
others say about you,
good or bad, or what you
say about yourself.
You are what you do.
Do good.
KEEP MOVING.

3

TRANSFORMATION

THE BLUE RUSHES IN

S ince I was a child, I have craved time alone. My parents joke that I spent the first eighteen years of my life in my bedroom—granted, I was frequently grounded for "sassing" them or fighting with my two younger sisters. But even when I wasn't banished to my room, I chose to go there. My books were there, and my art supplies, and my stereo—first a record player, then a tape deck, then a CD player. I would read and listen to the music I loved then, the music I still love now—the Beatles, the Cure, R.E.M., the Sundays, T. Rex. I would turn the record to side B, flip the tape, turn page after page after page.

I didn't realize how much I needed solitude—how restorative it is for me—until I had children. As the primary caregiver, I was rarely alone. I was used to having an audience always, even when I used the bathroom. When my son was a toddler, he'd play with his toys on the bathroom floor and talk to me while I took a bath. When he learned to read, he would bring in picture books and early readers, sit on the plush gray bath mat, and read to me, holding up the books while he read, like a teacher, so I could see the pictures.

Truth be told, he still wants to sit on the bath mat and talk to me. We play "the animal game" now—he thinks of an animal, and I, lounging in the suds, try to guess what it is.

"I'm thinking of an animal that lives in the ocean."

"Narwhal." (lathers hair)

"No."

"Anglerfish." (rinses hair)

"No."

"Orca." (squeezes conditioner into palm)

"Got it! Your turn."

I love that my children want to be with me—and I know enough about growing up to know that will change, and I should soak it up while I can—but I also have no trouble being alone for days on end. When I left my job in publishing in 2011 to freelance from home, people asked, "Aren't you worried you're going to get lonely? Aren't you going to miss having coworkers?"

I laughed. They didn't know me very well.

One afternoon, driving my son and daughter downtown to run errands, I sat at a traffic light—the corner of First Avenue and Summit—and watched as a couple of city workers cut down a dead tree. From the back seat, my daughter said something like, "I bet when they cut a tree down, the sky's like *finally*, and fills in the space."

"Yes!" I said. "And when you trim branches, the sky fills in before they even hit the ground."

"It's like when you pull your hand out of a bucket of water, and the water takes back the space."

I loved—still love—her mind.

My ex-husband and I had separated by then but were not yet divorced. I had bought some new furniture, rearranged some older pieces, hung new artwork. I was struck in that moment in the car: of course the sky rushes in when a tree is felled. It expands, taking up space it couldn't have before. It colors the space blue because now it can. The water takes back the hand-shaped space.

Let go of the narratives you've dragged around for years: you are not who you were as a child, or in year X, or on day Y—at least, not only. You do not have to fit yourself into those old, cramped stories. Be yourself here and now. KEEP MOVING.

Accept that you
may never get
to know what it
means. Accept that
there may not be a
reason, despite the
comfort that reasons
provide. Don't look
for meaning in
whatever collapsed
around you; make
meaning by digging
yourself out.

KEEP MOVING.

Reflect on what loss has given you, as counterintuitive as that sounds. Think of the solitude, self-reflection, and self-reliance as gifts. Of course they don't weigh the same as the grief— they don't balance the scales— but be grateful for them anyway.

KEEP MOVING.

Put one foot in front of the other and believe that the road will be there. Be proud: you are not only traveling a new road but making it as you go.

KEEP MOVING.

Think of what you've achieved that didn't seem possible last year, or five years ago, or ten; it didn't seem possible then but you've proven that it was. Now imagine what might be possible in another year or five or ten. KEEP MOVING.

Ask yourself what you would do if you had an unlimited supply of both courage and hope. Now begin answering that question with action. Take one step today—then repeat, repeat, repeat.

KEEP MOVING.

An empty space is full of potential. Believe that you are making room for something. Turn on the VACANCY sign.

KEEP MOVING.

Choose your words with a jeweler's eye, considering their facets, their clarity, their ability to reflect light. Speak without silencing others. Listen without losing your own voice.

KEEP MOVING.

n the summer of 2000, I moved in to my first apartment with the boyfriend I would later marry, then divorce. I was twenty-three years old, about to begin an MFA program, and he was twenty-two, starting his first postcollege job with the city arts council. In the fall of 2018, when he moved out of our house, we were both forty-one.

I had spent my entire adult life to that point with him. By that time, I was a freelance writer and editor; he was a lawyer. We had grown up together. What would I do now? Who would I be on my own?

Years ago, I read a book about metamorphosis with the kids. I knew the basic steps of the transformation—larva, chrysalis, butterfly—but I had no idea what happened inside a chrysalis to allow a caterpillar to exit a butterfly after what I'd assumed was a strange, shape-shifting nap. What I learned thrilled me: a caterpillar liquefies, then reconstitutes itself, becoming a different creature entirely.

The most fascinating part? The butterfly may actually carry in it knowledge—memories—from its first iteration. It is the same and yet it is completely different. It is itself and not. It carries inside it the old life while living the new one, which allows it to fly.

Acknowledge your desire for predictability—and think about how it competes with your sense of adventure, possibility, and surprise. Let yourself shrug. Let yourself be unsure.

KEEP MOVING.

You don't have
to be in love
to have love
in your life.
Take stock of
everything—
and everyone—
that fills
your heart.
KEEP MOVING.

Stop obsessing over the "lasts." Be ready to greet the firsts and yet-unseen nexts that are coming around the bend. Look alive—they'll be here any minute now.

KEEP MOVING.

Trust Future You
to handle some
of what Present
You is grappling
with. Future You
will know more
and hurt less.
Remember that
they're out there,
arms empty,
waiting to carry
what you hand
them.
KEEP MOVING.

When you think you know the shape and size of your life, when you think you know what is possible, something will happen to prove you wrong. Be open to this—you want to be wrong! Trust that your life is more elastic than you think: it can grow, be more, hold more.

KEEP MOVING.

Ask yourself how much of your self-image—what you believe to be real and true about yourself—is based on what others think of you. Allow yourself room to change. Let go of old narratives that no longer fit—or maybe they never did.

KEEP MOVING.

Sit with your doubt, your questions, your fear of the unknown, and do your best to be comfortable with them. Remember that you have no choice: knowing everything isn't an option. Don't compound your anxiety by being ashamed of it.

KEEP MOVING.

n 2019, I was contacted by a producer at the *Science of Happiness* podcast, a coproduction with the Greater Good Science Center at UC Berkeley. As a guest on the podcast, distributed by Public Radio International and PRX, I'd first choose a research-based practice for happiness, resilience, kindness, or connection from the Greater Good Science Center website. I'd try the practice for three weeks, and then I'd discuss my experience on the air. I'd liked that she referred to podcast guests as "Happiness Guinea Pigs."

The practice I chose was "Finding Silver Linings," labeled "moderate difficulty" on the website. It was a natural fit: I had been trying my best to find them for months. For ten minutes each day, I would jot down some things I was grateful for, then write about a recent negative experience, and finally list three "silver linings" to that dark experience.

Many of the negative experiences I wrote about were small, just pieces of a life in turmoil: a snarky text, an invoice from the lawyer, a professional disappointment. But I also started thinking on a larger scale. What were the silver linings—the unexpected perks—to being suddenly single? What had I gained through this loss, as counterintuitive as that sounds?

One thing immediately rose to the top of the list: solitude.

Since separating and negotiating joint custody, I have had more time to myself than I had in the previous twenty years. At first, life felt unnatural, like a tree with huge limbs lopped off, especially when the children were at their father's house. But as I sat with the discomfort, just learning to live with it, I listened to the silence around me. It was beautiful.

In the beginning, I treated every other weekend—the weekends the children were with their father—as a writing retreat. I drank too much coffee and wrote for hours, uninterrupted, the way I had in graduate school. I took long baths late at night, alone. I spent quality time with myself, filling in the space the way I wanted to.

Be creative not
only in your art
but in your life.
"That's the way
we've always done it"
is not reason
enough to keep
doing it that way.
Demand better.
Try something
new today.
Innovate. Play.

KEEP MOVING.

Let go of the idea that you could have done anything differently. But be confident that you know—and can do—better now. Watch the light negotiate its way through the leaves.

KEEP MOVING.

Revise the story you tell yourself about rejection. All that tells you is what you were worth to someone else—not what you are worth.

KEEP MOVING.

Good practice

for being loyal to

others is being loyal

to yourself; good

practice for being

honest with others

is being honest

with yourself.

Start with you.

KEEP MOVING.

Acknowledge what you have lost and what you are afraid of losing right now. Remember that you carry your home with you, because it *is* you. You are yours.

KEEP MOVING.

Think hard about what you want out of this year, next year, and into the wild, unknown future. Now name those things. Give them language. Write them down as a way of holding yourself accountable—not for achieving them, but for trying. Commit to trying.

KEEP MOVING.

The word *metamorphosis* comes from a Greek word that means "to change shape." When my marriage ended, my family changed shape, shrinking from a foursome to a threesome, reconstituting itself as something different but still recognizable.

My family is smaller now—it's me and the children, and occasionally it's just me—but in some ways my life has gotten larger, more expansive. I hadn't expected the blue to rush in like *finally*, but it did.

The blue is the self that had been patiently waiting, the self ready to be transformed.

As I fumble my way through being single in middle age, and being a single parent, I'm discovering that there is a difference between being alone and being lonely. Truly I'm neither. I live alone part of each week, but I still live in the city where I was born, and I have a large village: friends, family, neighbors, the literary community. I have a bundle of unconditional love here with me, too—a Boston terrier named Phoebe.

Even when I am alone—or at least without human company—I find the solitude energizing and recuperative. I'm grateful for it. Having this time alone has given me the opportunity to ask myself, *Who am I? What do I want?* I'm getting to know myself as an adult, an *I* who is no longer half of a *we*, and I am enjoying my own good company. A silver lining of being alone is being with someone you can trust, someone you respect and understand. You can let your guard down when you're by yourself. You can give yourself permission to live your authentic life, without apology. You can love yourself in a way that no one else can.

I am still learning this new life, and in many ways it still feels strange to me. I've begun filling the space that loss created around me. I can color the space around me however I want—*finally*—because now there is room. What I'm discovering is as surprising to me as the caterpillar's transformation: life on the other side of loss is not only livable but may be better, richer, more meaningful. I am more of myself for having gone through this strange and painful transformation, like entering the darkness and coming out with wings.

You are the same person you were before this grief, and yet you have been transformed by it. Both are true, as impossible as that sounds: you are the same and you are different. Let yourself be changed, and trust that change is not erasure.

KEEP MOVING.

Think about Pluto—how it continues to exist as itself, as always, oblivious to human categories. No one else gets to define you or determine your worth. Be a planet despite what they may call you.

KEEP MOVING.

Live with your fear, not inside it.

Do not mistake permission

to feel afraid in times of flux

as permission to cower.

Stand up. Uncover your eyes.

KEEP MOVING.

Let go of the idea that things could have happened differently, as if this life is a Choose Your Own Adventure book and you simply turned to the wrong page. You did the best you could with what you knew— and felt—at the time. Now do better, knowing more.

KEEP MOVING.

Stop conversing with
the noisy ghosts
in your head,
because winning an
imagined argument
isn't winning at all.
Say what you need
to say out loud or
on the page.
KEEP MOVING.

Know that the curiosity that drives you to create is the same curiosity that drives you toward the next part of your life. Let it lead you.

KEEP MOVING.

Celebrate your successes. Do not let grief or worry take that from you. Even as you carry darkness inside you, shine. Defy the darkness by shining.

KEEP MOVING.

Do not confuse tenderness with weakness. It is hard work to reach out instead of wrapping your arms around yourself as protection. Reach out today.

KEEP MOVING.

Rethink the words you use: *heartbroken, broken home, broken family.* In reclaiming the language, reclaim the narrative. You are not broken. Your family is not broken. Your life is not broken—it's changed shape and size.

KEEP MOVING.

Check your need
to control. If
you don't loosen
your grip, you
risk crushing
something
irreplaceable.
Let go. See what
happens next.

KEEP MOVING.

Setting down your anger toward someone doesn't mean excusing or forgiving them—it means protecting yourself. It means refusing to carry something that can poison you if you keep it close too long. Try to let go today, even just a little.

KEEP MOVING.

Remember how even when you can't see the moon, it's there. The moon isn't missing—it's only new. You are not gone, only changed. You're new.

KEEP MOVING.

come from a long line of women whose thoughts nest and stay. I hadn't thought about it this way until having children of my own and seeing myself in them. Parenting is like holding up a fun-house mirror—you see some of your best in your children, but you also see some of the rougher parts, exaggerated. I see my own worry, its face huge and distorted.

After my ex-husband moved out of the house, my son regressed. He expressed his sadness and anxiety as anger during the day and as fear at night. This child who had never needed a night-light was suddenly terrified to be left alone in his bedroom. I'd lie with him and try to fill him up with good thoughts: pancakes for breakfast on Saturday and gym tomorrow at school. Ice cream from that little shop at Holden Beach—Beaches -n- Cream—and hikes in Old Man's Cave. He'd say, "I'm trying to think the good thoughts, but the bad thoughts always push them out of the way."

I understood the power of "bad thoughts." For most of my life, even as a child, I used pessimism as self-protection. My thinking was this: *If I expect the worst and the worst doesn't happen, I will be pleasantly surprised. But if I expect the worst and the worst happens, not only will I be prepared but I will have been right.* I do so love to be right. I even thought that optimism was at odds with intelligence. It was so naïve to expect the best, wasn't it? Those people were bound for disappointment. Didn't they know how the world actually worked?

Think of yourself as a nesting doll: How many versions of yourself have you carried this far, to this point? How many more iterations will there be as you age? Know there is room for all of you.

KEEP MOVING.

Be careful not to poison yourself with your own anger, your own fear. Do one thing today to let in some light—that golden antivenin—instead. You cannot be cured of the darkness that's touched you, but you can survive it: can and will.

KEEP MOVING.

Accept the fact that some days burn, and you have to live them to get beyond them. There's no way to the other side but through. Go through. Walk the hot coals but don't look down at your feet. Look ahead.

KEEP MOVING.

What hurt yesterday
will hurt today
and tomorrow, but
over time the sharp
pain may dull to
an ache. Trust that
you will learn how
to move—and
live—with the ache,
that you will be
transformed by it in
ways you can't yet
imagine.

KEEP MOVING.

There is nothing
you need to do
differently to
be lovable—no
emotional debt
you have to pay,
no change you
have to make.
Know this like
you know your
own voice, your
own pulse.

KEEP MOVING.

once wrote in a poem that the future is empty. The poem was inspired by one of those questions my daughter asked me when she was in preschool.

FUTURE

What is the future?

Everything that hasn't happened yet, the future
is tomorrow and next year and when you're old
but also in a minute or two, when I'm through
answering. The future is nothing I imagined
as a child: no jet packs, no conveyor-belt sidewalks,
no bell-jarred cities at the bottom of the sea.
The trick of the future is that it's empty,
a cup before you pour the water. The future
is a waiting cup, and for all it knows, you'll fill it
with milk instead. You're thirsty. Every minute
carries you forward, conveys you, into a space
you fill. I mean the future will be full of you.
It's one step beyond the step you're taking now.
What you'll say next until you say it.

What I mean is that the future is empty even though we tell ourselves we've already filled it. We plan as if somehow those mental blueprints fill the future. We have to imagine some control over the future so that we can bear going there, into "the great wild beyond," but the truth is, it's impossible to predict. The life you've lived for the past five, ten, or twenty years may not be the life you live five, ten, or twenty years from now. The partner you expect to be there may or may not be there. The work you do now may change. The money you're saving, the house you're paying down, the apartment you hope to keep, the children you're raising . . .

You see what I mean. Is this freeing or heartbreaking? Comforting or terrifying? All of it, all at once?

When I was married, I'd thought of my future as being full. I imagined growing old with this person. I imagined our kids growing up, going off to college. I wondered if we would downsize when they moved out, or if we'd keep the house so the kids and their families would have a place to sleep when they visited us.

But the future had always been empty. The future is no emptier for me now than it was when I was married. It's no less uncertain. There was never a guarantee that we would stay together, or that either of us would live a long life. There was no guarantee that we would be in rocking chairs on a porch somewhere, talking about our grandchildren.

The difference between my married future and my future alone is just that: I alone have to reimagine, re-envision—yes, revise—what might fill it. This life is no longer a group project.

Be as accommodating
with yourself as you
are with the people
you love. Do not
hold yourself to some
impossible standard.
Cut yourself some slack:
you are human, and you
are trying.

KEEP MOVING.

The only way to avoid grief is to opt out—to refuse to invest in your work or your relationships, to avoid loving anything you could lose. If you want to be all in, you are showing up for all of it—the joy and the pain.

KEEP MOVING.

Revise the story
you tell yourself
about failure.
Consider yourself
an apprentice in
the world. Learn
all you can. Gain
experience.
KEEP MOVING.

Raise your antenna and tune in. Ignore the static and turn your dial to a kinder frequency. Call it whatever you want— spirit, life force, the universe, the soul, God— but know it's there. Listen closely. Pay attention.

KEEP MOVING.

The best way to
prepare for the
future is to be
present. The best
indicator of future
peace is peace in
the present. You
can't know what
will happen, but
you can ready
yourself.

KEEP MOVING.

When something hurts, instead of distracting yourself, instead of trying to fix it or cover it up, just pay attention. Focus. Feel it. Trust that it will pass.

KEEP MOVING.

Even if you haven't been forgiven, forgive. Even if you haven't been treated with care, treat others with care. Even if you've been wronged, commit to doing right.

KEEP MOVING.

MAGGIE SMITH

S omething unexpected—and, frankly, life-altering—happened when my marriage ended: I realized that I could no longer afford to be a pessimist. I could no longer allow my worst thoughts to gather twigs and ribbons and make a permanent home in my mind.

I realized pessimism wasn't going to get me out of bed, or get the coffee made, or pack the kids' lunches, or do the laundry, or make my deadlines. Pessimism wasn't going to help me or my children. And so, in a very dark time, it occurred to me that being optimistic moment by moment was a gift I could give myself. Even if whatever I'm hoping for doesn't materialize, I am feeding my spirit in the meantime. I am not poisoning the present with worry or despair or defeatist thinking.

Today I think of myself as a "recovering pessimist." I know that optimism is not at odds with wisdom. It's quite the opposite. I think of cynicism as cool but lazy, while hope is desperately uncool—it has sweaty palms and an earnest smile on its face. What I know to be true is that one hopeful person will accomplish more than a hundred cynics. Why? Because the hopeful person will *try*.

Think about origin stories. Imagine that whatever you're going through now is the key to your powers. Set your mind on transformation.

KEEP MOVING.

Do not bargain away
pieces of yourself for
approval. It's a bad deal.
If there are conditions on
someone's love for you,
understand: that is not
love. Move on.

KEEP MOVING.

Do not hold yourself to some impossible standard. The word *amateur* comes from the Latin *amare*, meaning "to love." Let yourself be a beginner, an amateur—someone who is learning to live a new life, someone who loves it for its potential.

KEEP MOVING.

Being creative—
creating, making
from scratch—
applies not only
to your work but
to your life. Be
creative in your
daily life. Practice
the qualities of a
creative person:
observant,
innovative, open.
KEEP MOVING.

Do not sit still inside your grief, your fear. Take one step toward making something real and lasting, something you can be proud of. Maybe that something is you.

KEEP MOVING.

Remember when
you would have
been over-the-moon
thrilled to have just
a fraction of your
life as it is now?
Look around you:
it is enough.
KEEP MOVING.

've written that the future is empty, but I could say it another way: the future is full of nothing but possibility.

Again, is that freeing or heartbreaking? Comforting or terrifying? The next five minutes of your life can be one thing or a million other things. You can choose to keep reading this book or not. (Are you still here? I hope you're still here.) You can make tea or you can take a walk. You can tell someone you love them or you can tell someone it's over. You can put your house on the market. You can go back to school or start looking for a new job. You can decide to love the job you have, the person who sleeps beside you, the person you see in the mirror.

The future is empty: How will you fill it?

What kinds of thoughts will nest in you?

Despite grief and uncertainty, despite trauma and loss—collective and personal—I carry hope with me. I hope you do, too. I hope you're pushing forward, refusing to go back to the cluttered past. Yes, the past is full—a hoard—and some of the things back there bring us comfort, because they are familiar. But we cannot go back there. Even my kids know this—once you turn six, there's no being five again.

My daughter's third-grade teacher, Mrs. Allen, talked a lot about what she called "the power of *yet.*" She'd tell the kids, "You have not learned that . . . yet." She'd say, "You don't know how to do that . . . yet." I think about this now, as I create a new life for myself. I'm not at home in this life . . . yet. I'm not healed from the pain of divorce . . . yet. But living is a hopeful act in itself. It's a choice we make daily: to be. To keep being.

I'm apprenticing myself to hope and learning as much as I can. I'm making space in my mind for the good thoughts, so they can nestle in and sing.

ACKNOWLEDGMENTS

Thank you to Julia Cheiffetz at One Signal Publishers and to Joy Tutela at the David Black Literary Agency for believing in this book from the beginning. You are both powerhouses and wonderful humans.

Gratitude to Kelly Sundberg, Annie McGreevy, and Victoria Chang, whose feedback on this project was instrumental.

Tyler Meier and Patri Hadad at the University of Arizona Poetry Center, and Sandy Coomer at Rockvale Writers' Colony, generously provided the time and space in which parts of this book came together. Thank you.

Biggest thanks to the family and friends who supported me during this difficult time: especially Nita Smith, Steve Smith, Katie Riley, Carly Debnam, Lisa Rovner, Jennifer Riley, Ann Townsend, Kelly Sundberg, and Amy Butcher.

"Future" from *Good Bones*, published by Tupelo Press, copyright © 2017 by Maggie Smith. Used with permission.

A portion of "The Golden Repair" was adapted from my essay "Here Comes the Sun," originally published in *Mothering Through the Darkness: Women Open Up About the Postpartum Experience* (She Writes Press, 2015).

"Nesters" was adapted from a letter I wrote for *The Rumpus* subscription series "Letters in the Mail."

"After the Fire" references research by Lawrence G. Calhoun and Richard Tedeschi (Posttraumatic Growth Research Group, Department of Psychology, UNC Charlotte, https://ptgi.uncc.edu/ptg-research-group/), and an article by Jean Rhodes and Mary Waters ("You've Heard of Post-Traumatic Stress, but What about Post-Traumatic Growth?" *Scientific American*, September 24, 2018, https://blogs.scientificamerican.com/observations/youve-heard-of-post -traumatic-stress-but-what-about-post-traumatic-growth/).